WILDLIFE HOTSPO...
National Parks, Nature Reserves a...

Ards Forest Park

Glenariff Forest Park

Glenveagh National Park

Drum Manor Forest Park

Rossmore Forest Park

Tollymore Forest Park

Slieve Gullion Forest Park

Ballycroy National Park

Hazelwood

Lough Key Forest Park

Oldhead Wood Nature Reserve

Dún na Rí Forest Park

Connemara National Park

Phoenix Park

Donadea Forest Park

Wicklow Mountains National Park

Portumna Forest Park

The Burren National Park

Caher Forest Park

Curraghchase Forest Park

Tintern Abbey

Killarney Forest Park

Gougane Barra Forest Park

To Fiona,
Best wishes,

Juanita Browne

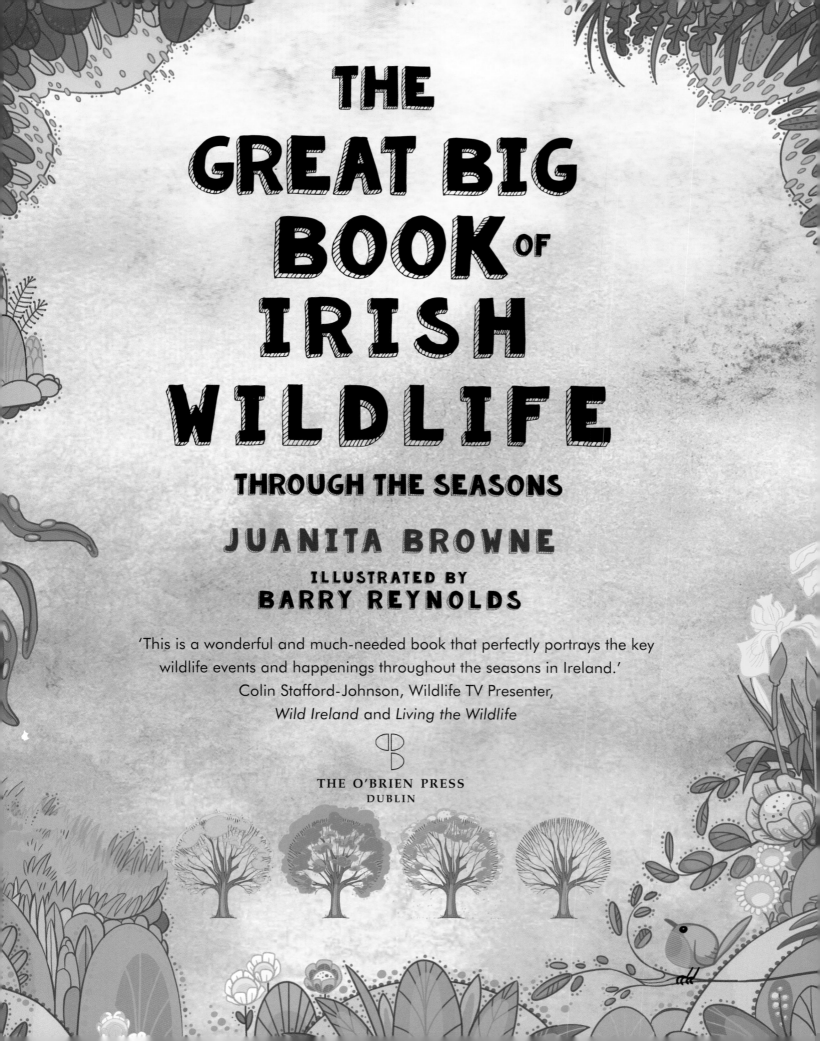

THE GREAT BIG BOOK OF IRISH WILDLIFE

THROUGH THE SEASONS

JUANITA BROWNE

ILLUSTRATED BY
BARRY REYNOLDS

'This is a wonderful and much-needed book that perfectly portrays the key wildlife events and happenings throughout the seasons in Ireland.'
Colin Stafford-Johnson, Wildlife TV Presenter,
Wild Ireland and *Living the Wildlife*

THE O'BRIEN PRESS
DUBLIN

ABOUT THE AUTHOR

I always loved animals so when I went to college I studied zoology. I enjoy sharing stories about wildlife and the natural world, and have worked on wildlife magazines and books, such as *Ireland's Mammals* and *My First Book of Irish Animals*. I also make natural history documentaries for television and radio, including *The Secret Life of the Shannon* and *Wild Ireland*.
My latest job involves working with the National Biodiversity Data Centre, on an exciting project called the All-Ireland Pollinator Plan – conserving bees, bumblebees and the wildflowers and hedgerows they depend on. There is always more to learn about nature. I'm still learning every day!

Juanita

ABOUT THE ILLUSTRATOR

Dubliner Barry Reynolds is a character designer, visual development and storyboard artist and illustrator who has worked on the Oscar-nominated animated movie *The Secret of Kells*, on Aardman and Sony Pictures Animation's *Arthur Christmas*, on various Disney TV shows and on Irish language graphic novels, *An Táin* and *Deirdre agus Mic Uisnigh*, where his artwork helped bring these Irish legends to a new readership. As a child, Barry saw *The Jungle Book* and announced then that he intended to be an artist, and he has realised that dream, apart from a few brief flirtations with wanting to be an astronaut, a dinosaur hunter and a zoologist … the last of which came in handy when working on *The Great Big Book of Irish Wildlife*.

Barry Reynolds

CONTENTS

THE STORY OF IRISH NATURE THROUGH THE YEAR

This book is a little like a diary for our animals and plants over the course of one year. Nature changes with the seasons. For example each spring, many birds have their chicks; while in autumn, our forests' leaves change colour and fall from their branches.

Nature is amazing and it is all around us. But nature is also very complex and there are too many different Irish plants, insects, birds and animals to fit in one book. Most of the animals and plants in this book are easy to find in a garden or park or at the seashore, while others might need a special effort – such as a boat trip to see dolphins or nesting seabirds on an offshore island.

Orange-tip butterfly

NATURE'S CALENDAR

In Ireland, the calendar tells us that winter runs from December to February; spring is March to May; summer is June to August; and autumn refers to the months of September to November. But nature doesn't use the human calendar! Instead, animals and plants respond to factors like daylight length and temperature: hedgehogs wake up from hibernation in spring, but the timing depends on the temperature; and frogs usually lay their eggs in spring. As we go through the year, we will see why things happen when they do and the reasons why nature needs to change with the seasons.

Hedgehog

Frogs can spawn as early as January if the weather is mild.

Grey seals

HOW THE BOOK WORKS

The four sections of this book follow our seasons: spring, summer, autumn and winter.
Each section explores:

- ➤ The changes in that season and some of the animals and plants you can see. Many can be seen all year round, but they might be easier to see in certain seasons, for instance hares are more visible in early spring when the grass is short.
- ➤ The most exciting Irish wildlife events of each season, such as when large numbers of grey seals gather on our offshore islands to give birth each autumn, or when seabirds form colonies to rear their young in summer.
- ➤ Activities you can try for yourself, like feeding the birds that visit your garden in winter, or visiting a seashore to investigate life in our rock pools.

Puffins

The Cliffs of Moher, Co. Clare

Glenveagh National Park, Co. Donegal

PLACES TO VISIT

Wildlife can be found anywhere and everywhere – if you know how to look. In Ireland, we have lots of wonderful wildlife and different habitats, such as ocean, seashore, mountains, lakes, bogs, forests, and even your back garden or schoolyard. This book suggests places you can visit and groups you can join, to help you track down Irish wildlife.

The Great Big Book of Irish Wildlife is a celebration of the variety and beauty around us, from the amazing super powers that some of our animals have – like our bats who can find their way in the pitch dark using their super hearing or our spiders who spin webs that are stronger than steel – to our smaller, more secret, natural wonders, such as tiny flowers, ants, ladybirds and woodlice.

I hope this book helps to show you how to enjoy the Irish countryside and its special animals and plants.

Let's get started!

SPRING

In spring, the natural world comes to life after winter.

WAKING UP

Trees and hedgerows reveal new buds, which will become young green leaves, and early spring flowers start to bloom, such as lesser celandine, primroses and dandelions.

Bluebells in woodland, Wicklow National Park

BIRDLIFE

Birds become very active, as spring is when most of them breed. Many male birds show off their brightly coloured feathers to attract females. Some birds perform courtship displays in the air or on the water and use mating calls to attract a mate. After the female chooses her mate, they start to build a nest for their new family.

Songbirds, including the goldfinch, sing loudly at dawn and dusk during spring. May is the month when the *dawn chorus* is at its loudest, with birds singing from before 4am – before the sun is even up! Males sing to impress the girls and tell other birds 'this is my patch'.

MAMMALS AND INSECTS

Animals that have been hibernating, such as hedgehogs and bats, begin to wake up once temperatures rise again and the insects they feed on start to appear.

DID YOU KNOW?

In spring, insects are on the wing again. Huge bumblebee queens fly about on warm days as they search for a new nest site.

Whitethorn is also called the 'May bush' because of its pretty white flowers that bloom in May. Mayfly emerge from our rivers and lakes in May. They live for only one more day when they mate and lay their eggs in water, before becoming food for fish and birds.

The cockchafer or Maybug beetle can be seen (or heard flying into windows) in late April and early May.

Bumblebee

A mayfly on whitethorn/hawthorn

Cockchafer

ARRIVALS AND DEPARTURES

Birds that come to Ireland to spend the winter here – the geese, swans and waders – leave our shores in spring, to raise their families back home. They will fly back again to Ireland next autumn.

Other birds arrive to spend the summer here: sand martin and wheatear come from Africa, from mid-March, followed by house martin, swift, swallow, and cuckoo in April and May.

The sighting of the first swallow is a sign that summer is on its way.

SPRING IN THE GARDEN

Spring gardens attract insects and birds looking for nest sites and food.

Country gardens may be home to rabbits and foxes; gardens close to woodland may be visited by hedgehogs and deer; if you live near water, frogs may be hiding in your lawn.

URBAN WILDLIFE

You can encourage plenty of birds, butterflies and bees to come calling by planting pollen-rich flowers and shrubs; making homes for wildlife, such as nestboxes; or by providing food. Pollinators, such as bumblebees, love the nectar of honeysuckle, buddleia, sedum, dandelions and lavender. Fruit trees and wildflowers, such as clover, are also great for bees. Lots of birds use buildings for their homes, too, nesting under the roof or in the walls.

Foxes often live alongside humans in urban areas and can be spotted at dawn and dusk.

IN THE DARK OF NIGHT

Many of our animals are nocturnal; they become active at night, looking for food, and rest during the day, keeping safe from predators and humans.

Rabbits may use your lawn after dark when they feel it is safe to leave their underground warren.

BABY BIRD MONTH

May is baby-bird month and this is super timing as there are plenty of caterpillars for the busy birds to bring back to their nestlings.

Have you noticed that different birds have favourite places in your garden where they build their nests?

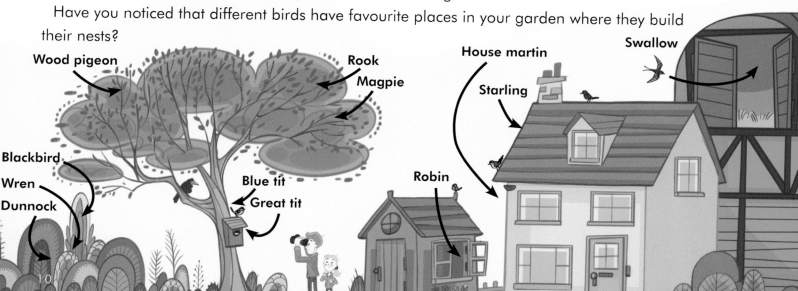

Wood pigeon
Rook
Magpie
House martin
Swallow
Starling
Blackbird
Wren
Dunnock
Blue tit
Great tit
Robin

BLUE TIT

Blue tits are very pretty, busy little birds you see in most gardens.

NESTING TIME

In spring, blue tits begin looking for nest sites. When the male finds a spot, he flutters his wings and calls to attract a female to the site. If she is happy with the nest site, she starts to build the nest, collecting dried grass, moss and dead leaves, to form the cup-shaped nest. Then she lines the nest with soft feathers, moss or fur she finds. It can take up to 2 weeks to build a nest.

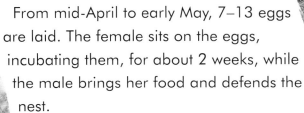

From mid-April to early May, 7–13 eggs are laid. The female sits on the eggs, incubating them, for about 2 weeks, while the male brings her food and defends the nest.

The chicks have no feathers and are blind when they hatch, so they are totally dependent on their parents. Both parents feed their young chicks, mainly with caterpillars.

After about 3 weeks spent growing and getting their feathers, the chicks learn to fly.

DID YOU KNOW?

Blue tit parents must feed their chicks up to 500 times a day. That's 500 dinners to find!

ABOUT ME - BLUE TIT

My Irish name: *Meantán gorm*.
I like to eat: Caterpillars, small insects, seeds and peanuts.
My voice: I make a high-pitched 'tsee-hee-he-hee' song.
Home: I nest in holes in trees, buildings and nest boxes in woodlands, gardens, parks and hedgerows.

SPRING FLOWERS

Wildflowers bring colour to the countryside once more.

Primroses are one of the first flowers to bloom each year — from January to June.

Bluebells have flowers shaped like small bells and appear in our woodlands in April and May — before the tree canopy closes over and reduces the light that can reach plants on the forest floor.

Speedwell is a pretty little blue flower that grows in grassy places. It flowers from March to July and was used to make a cough medicine.

Wood anemone and **ramsons** are also found on the woodland floor in spring. Ramsons are also called **'wild garlic'** and make the forest smell of garlic! (Main background picture.)

Dandelions appear in gardens and on roadside verges from early spring. Gardeners are not keen on them, but they provide bees and other insects with nectar and pollen.

Buttercups have shiny yellow flowers that can be enjoyed from April to October. If you hold a buttercup under someone's chin and it makes their skin shine yellow, the saying goes that they like eating butter.

Daffodils are beautiful early flowers of parks and gardens.

Lesser celandines grow in woodlands, grassy banks and meadows, and you can see them on roadsides from February to May. They are bright yellow, but have thinner petals and more of them than the buttercup.

In May, **cow parsley** is in bloom and lines our roadsides.

Wood sorrel is a pretty spring woodland flower with large shamrock-shaped leaves.

Cowslips have bunches of lovely yellow flowers. Another name for cowslips are 'keys', as it was said that they are St Peter's keys for the gates of Heaven that he dropped to earth.

DID YOU KNOW?

The magic number!
Once temperatures hit the magic number of 7°C, plants begin to grow again, including grasses, so gardeners have to get mowing.

A FROG'S LIFE

A frog is an amphibian; it begins its life in water and then, spends most of its time on land.

Each spring – but sometimes as early as January or February depending on the weather – frogs return to the same pond in which they were born, to breed and lay their eggs (this is called **spawning**).

Males usually arrive at the pond first and croak loudly at night to call the females.

Each female lays about 2,000 eggs which are fertilised by a male. The eggs then take in water and swell up to form **frogspawn** that floats on the surface.

After about 2 weeks, a tadpole wriggles out of each egg.

After about 5 weeks, its back legs grow. It now breathes air and must swim to the surface to take gulps of air.

At about 10 weeks, it grows front legs, too. Then its tail begins to disappear as it is absorbed back into its body.

Soon the tadpole has become a **froglet**, which looks like a perfect miniature frog. Froglets leave the pond in June or July to begin life on land.

Frogspawn

DID YOU KNOW?

The transformation from tadpole to frog is called metamorphosis.

Frogs can live for 7 or 8 years.

Frogs come in lots of colours – from yellow to pale green to dark brown.

A frog's skin can become darker to match its surroundings – to camouflage it and make it more difficult for predators, like herons, hedgehogs and rats, to find.

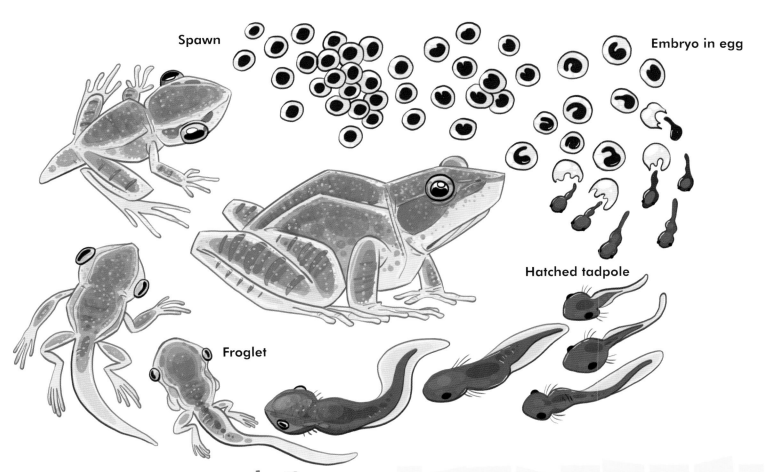

Spawn

Embryo in egg

Hatched tadpole

Froglet

What do you get when you cross a frog with a sheep? A woolly jumper!

This colour change takes about two hours.
The common frog is the only species of frog in Ireland.
There are two other amphibians in Ireland – the rare natterjack toad, only found in counties Kerry and Wexford, and the smooth newt.

ABOUT ME - FROG

My Irish name: *Frog.*

My body: I have webbed feet to help me swim fast.

My eyes are very sensitive to movement. When small insects move close by, I flick out my long tongue to grab my dinner.

My long sticky tongue is attached to the front of my mouth (instead of the back like yours!). My tongue can be a third the length of my body. If you had the same sort of tongue it would reach your belly button!

I like to eat: Insects, worms, spiders and slugs, making me very popular with gardeners.

Home: In wetlands, ponds, damp vegetation and hedgerows.

`MAD AS A MARCH HARE`
The Irish mountain hare is unique to Ireland.

There is an old saying 'as mad as a March hare'. This is because March is the best time to see hares in the short spring grass – jumping about, chasing each other, and leap-frogging and boxing with their front paws. This is **courtship** behaviour when males are chasing females, and they do this throughout much of the year.

The Irish mountain hare does not usually turn white in winter, unlike other mountain hares in parts of the world where there is more snow.

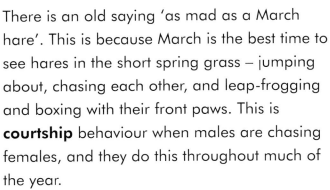

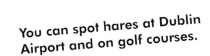

You can spot hares at Dublin Airport and on golf courses.

Boxing hares

16

What do you call a group of hares creeping slowly backwards? A receding hare-line!

HARE HABITAT

Rabbits live in underground burrows called a warren. Hares live above ground and have leverets in **forms**, dips in the ground.

DID YOU KNOW?

Male hares are called jacks, females are jills and babies are leverets.

Hares are usually nocturnal but can be active during spring days.

They do not dig burrows like rabbits; they rest in a shallow dip in the ground called a form.

ABOUT ME – HARE

My Irish name: *Giorria*.

My body: I am bigger than a rabbit, with longer legs and ears. My hind feet are very long and I can run very fast – up to 50 kilometres per hour.

I like to eat: Grasses, heather, and herbs, also gorse, willow, bilberry and other shrubs.

Home: Open farmland, uplands, bogs and grasslands.

BADGER

The badger is a beautiful, nocturnal animal with black stripes on its face.

Badgers live in woodland and under hedgerows. Their home is called a **sett.** The sett is a long network of tunnels and sleeping chambers that can cover hundreds of metres underground and have many entrances.

SPRING

Badgers live in family groups. In early spring, badger cubs are born below ground in a cosy chamber lined with dried grass. They are fed with mother's milk.

When they are about seven weeks old, they start to come above ground at night with their parents to explore the world and to learn how to find food. Cubs also spend a lot of time playing and wrestling with each other.

SUMMER

Hot dry weather can make life difficult for badgers as the ground gets very hard and earthworms go deeper into the soil, making it more work for badgers to catch their dinner.

AUTUMN

In autumn, badgers eat as much as they can to help them get through the winter. They make the most of the autumn berries and mushrooms.

A badger sett

DID YOU KNOW?

The male badger is a **boar**, the female a **sow**, and the young are **cubs**. The badger has five strong claws on each foot to help dig for food, and to dig tunnels. Badgers are clean animals and have their toilet outside the sett. Next to man, badgers build the largest homes in the world, but their homes are underground!

WINTER

During winter, badgers become less active, spending more time underground, and on cool days their body temperature drops, in a process called **torpor**, so that they use less energy. But badgers do not hibernate. Hibernation is a much more extended form of torpor.

ABOUT ME - BADGER

My Irish name: *Broc.*
Length: **90cm.**
Weight: **9–15kg. (Boars are bigger than sows.)**
I like to eat: **I am an omnivore. I eat plants and animals, such as my favourite earthworms, and beetles, snails, slugs, frogs, fungi, fruit, cereals and small mammals.**

SPRING ON THE RIVERBANK

OTTER

The otter usually lives alone. It marks its territory with its droppings, called **spraints**. If you see more than one otter, it is probably a mother and her cubs.

Otters breed in spring, and after 9 weeks, 2 or 3 cubs are born. They stay with their mother for 6 months to a year, learning how to catch fish.

River Shannon

DID YOU KNOW?

The otter is an excellent swimmer and has webbed toes to help it swim.

The otter has a double fur coat. A dense layer of underfur traps air to keep the skin dry, and an outer layer of guard hairs helps to keep it warm.

The otter's long stiff whiskers help it sense movements in the water made by fish.

ABOUT ME - OTTER

My Irish name: Madra uisce, which means 'water dog'.

Length: Males 90cm; females 80cm, plus 30–40cm of tail!

Weight: 7–11kg.

I like to eat: Fish, crayfish, and small mammals.

Home: I make a burrow in the riverbank, called a holt. My holt has a number of entrances, some underwater.

DIPPER

The dipper hunts for small insects underwater. Its name comes from how it dips its body up and down.

KINGFISHER

The kingfisher is one of our most colourful birds and is also a master fisherman. It sits patiently on a branch overlooking the water, and when it spots a fish, it dives headfirst under the surface. It flies back to the branch carrying its dinner, and either swallows it whole or carries it back to his nest to feed to its chicks.

DID YOU KNOW?

Kingfishers dig a tunnel – about 1m long – in the side of a steep riverbank so that predators can't reach it, and it is here they make their nest.

GREY HERON

The grey heron can stand like a **statue** for hours on end, waiting for fish to pass under its shadow. Then it strikes suddenly with its long sharp, dagger-like bill.

REEDS

Reeds offer nesting places for many birds such as the sedge warbler, coot, moorhen and grebes.

YELLOW FLAG IRIS

The yellow flag or yellow iris is a beautiful, tall spring flower of wet places, with stripes on its yellow petals that act as **nectar guides** to help insects find their way into the flower.

21

FOX

The fox is a very clever wild dog.

DID YOU KNOW?

The male fox is called a dog; the female is called a vixen; and the young are called cubs.

The fox's hearing is one of its best hunting tools, helping it find its dinner. Its large ears even help it hear earthworms or mice moving through grass. Foxes don't bark. They are usually very quiet, but in winter, their breeding season, and spring you might hear the males and females using sharp, high-pitched shrieks. These calls can sound like scary screams and may have led to tales of the Irish ghost, the banshee.

A fox couple may stay together for a number of years. Their cubs are born each spring in an underground **den** or **earth**. For the first few weeks, the vixen stays with her cubs and the dog helps his family by finding food. Sometimes an **aunt**, a female from a previous litter will help rear the cubs. Fox cubs start to come above ground in late spring, and can be seen playing near their den.

Apart from when they have small cubs, foxes usually don't use an underground earth. Instead they 'lie up' above ground, staying hidden during the day, and coming out at night to hunt.

Food storage

What do you call a fox wearing ear muffs? Anything you like – he can't hear you!

ABOUT ME - FOX

My Irish name: *Sionnach/madra rua*, which means 'red dog'.

Length from my nose to the tip of my tail: 100cm.

My tail measures 40cm!

Weight: 6–9kg.

I like to eat: Lots of different foods, including mice, rats, rabbits, birds, eggs and dead animals. But I also like insects, earthworms and fruits such as blackberries and apples.

MASTERS OF THE NIGHT SKY

**Owls are master night-time hunters of shrews, mice, voles, and rats.
They have a wonderful sense of hearing.**

BARN OWL

The barn owl is nocturnal. It sleeps during the day and hunts at night.
A male and female barn owl often pair for life. Between April and May they lay a clutch of 4–7 eggs. After about a month, the eggs hatch. The parents go out to hunt at night and on a good night they will catch more than 25 small mammals to bring back to the nest. After about 12 weeks the young owls learn to fly and become independent.

ABOUT ME - BARN OWL

My Irish name: Scréachóg reilige, which means 'graveyard screecher', because I have a high-pitched call and I nest in old churches, castles and other ruined buildings.

DID YOU KNOW?

The feathers on the barn owl's face help to focus soundwaves – like a satellite dish – towards its ears so that it can track its prey, even in the pitch dark.

The barn owls' feathers are very soft – another adaptation for quiet flight.

Almost-silent flight allows barn owls to hear the quiet sounds produced by their small mammal prey and approach them undetected.

LONG-EARED OWLS

You can see why the long-eared owl got this name. But these are not actually ears, but tufts of feathers. The ear tufts are raised when the owl is alarmed or curious, but lie flat when the owl is relaxed or flying.

Long-eared owls nest early in the year, from March onwards. They usually nest in trees – in the old stick nests of crows or magpies. They incubate their eggs for about a month, and the chicks learn to fly at about 5 weeks old. The chicks stay in the trees around the nest, and depend on their parents until they are about 2 months old.

DID YOU KNOW?

Long-eared owls are the most common owl in Ireland. There is probably a nest near your house! But they are very difficult to find.

The best time of year to find them is spring when they have chicks – because the chicks have a loud call like a high-pitched squeaky gate.

ABOUT ME – LONG-EARED OWL

My Irish name: Ceann cait, means 'cat head' because my ear tuft feathers make my face look a little like a cat's.

WILDLIFE FUN IN SPRING

**As the weather becomes warmer and days longer,
you can spot lots of wildlife.**

KEEP A WILDLIFE DIARY

Record in a notebook what birds, flowers, mammals and mini-beasts you spot. You can make sketches, stick in photographs, dried leaves or pressed flowers, to make it a wonderful wildlife scrapbook.

WHAT TO SPOT

Frogspawn: Visit a pond to look for frogspawn. You can send your sightings to the Irish Peatland Conservation Council 'Hop To It Frog' Survey, on www.ipcc.ie/a-to-z-peatlands/frogs.

Nestbuilders: In spring, watch for signs of nest-building, as birds carry moss, twigs and other nesting material. You can help by leaving pet fur or straw on a bird table. You could also record which materials are the most popular.

Below left: House martin feeding a chick in its nest, made of mud. Below right: Long-tailed tit peeking out of its nest of lichens and moss.

Swallows arriving in spring

Spring flowers: Visit a bluebell wood, such as Lough Key Forest Park, Co. Roscommon or Glen of the Downs, Co. Wicklow, to catch this amazing floral display. See pages 12–13 for some of our beautiful spring flowers to spot and the map showing some Irish woodlands to visit.

Mini-beasts: We have 21 different bumblebees in Ireland – learn how to be a Bumblebee Recorder, identifying bees and sending your sightings to the National Biodiversity Data Centre, www.biodiversityireland.ie. You can also plant wildflowers and shrubs in your garden to attract bumblebees. (See www.pollinators.ie)

THE NATIONAL DAWN CHORUS

National Dawn Chorus events are organised by BirdWatch Ireland, around the first Sunday in May. (See www.birdwatchireland.ie) Bird experts will help you identify which birds are singing.

NATIONAL BIODIVERSITY WEEK

National Biodiversity Week takes place towards the end of May to celebrate wildlife, with bat walks, bog tours and wildlife talks happening all over the country, see www.biodiversityweek.ie. Check out what events are planned by wildlife organisations, such as the Irish Wildlife Trust, www.iwt.ie; Bat Conservation Ireland, www.batconservationireland.org; Irish Peatland Conservation Council, www.ipcc.ie; and Irish Whale and Dolphin Group, www.iwdg.ie.

SUMMER

Many animals raise their young in the summer months.

Wildflower meadow, Killarney, Co. Kerry

Pyramidal orchid

MAMMALS

Fallow deer give birth in summer. You can see fallow deer with their **fawns** in the Phoenix Park in Dublin.

Badgers cubs, born underground in spring, spend the summer nights exploring the world above ground, learning to find food.

Fox cubs can be seen playing outside their den on long summer days.

HARBOUR OR COMMON SEAL

Harbour seals give birth around July. The pup looks like a miniature version of its mum, and already has waterproof fur and blubber to keep it warm, so it car start to swim from the day it is born.

Cormorant

SEABIRDS

On coastal walks and boat trips, many different seabirds can be spotted breeding on the cliffs.

INSECTS AND SPIDERS

Summer is the season when insect numbers are at their highest – both the flying ones and the ones hiding in the grass, trees and hedges.

Birds raise their chicks on all the flying insects, spiders and caterpillars that appear at this time of year.

Keep an eye out for **dragonflies** and **damselflies** near streams and ponds as they lay their eggs in water.

Honeybees collect nectar from flowers and turn it into honey in their hives. You can see bees using their long tongues to suck up the sweet nectar. They collect pollen in **pollen baskets** on their back legs, bringing it back to the hive to feed to the baby bees.

All our bees, including the beautiful fat and furry bumblebees, and our **hoverflies,** are important pollinators. While the bee is collecting pollen and nectar from a flower, some of the flower's pollen rubs onto its body and the bee carries it to the next flower. This is called pollination and allows plants to produce seeds and fruits to grow.

Dragonfly

DID YOU KNOW?

Plants grow 10 times faster in July than they do in February.

Ireland has 1 honeybee and 98 types of wild bee, including 77 solitary bees and 21 bumblebees.

To make just one jar of honey, 1,000 honeybees must visit 4.5 million flowers!

Honeybees do a little dance to show other bees in their hive which direction they should fly in to find the best nectar.

SUMMER IN THE GARDEN

In summer our gardens are full of life and colour.

Visiting butterflies bring colour to our gardens. **Buddleia**, or the 'butterfly bush', is a shrub that attracts butterflies.

We enjoy lots of flowers in summer, such as **foxglove** (See right), which you will see in gardens and woodlands and on roadsides between May and September.

DID YOU KNOW?

We have 20 types of ladybird in Ireland. Ladybirds hide their wings under hard, colourful wing cases. They pull back these wing cases and unfold their wings before they fly away. Gardeners like ladybirds because they eat aphids – small insects that damage their plants.

CUCKOO SPIT

You might see strange bubbly goo sticking to plant stems in summer. This is called cuckoo spit but it has nothing to do with the cuckoo! It's made by the grub of an insect called a **froghopper.** The froghopper feeds on the juices of plants and makes bubbles with its bottom! It hides inside the 'cuckoo spit' until it becomes an adult.

SWALLOWS AND HOUSE MARTINS

Swallows and house martins arrive in Ireland in summer. Swallows nest in open barns and sheds, while house martins nest under the eaves of houses. They both swoop through the air, hunting flying insects.

DID YOU KNOW?

Swallows and house martins spend the winter in southern Africa. In spring, they fly 10,000km and cross the Sahara Desert to spend the summer in Ireland. They fly about 300km each day during this migration.

BATS

Summary is a busy time for our bats as they have their babies.

Between June and July, bats gather in a **maternity roost** and the female gives birth to one baby bat, called a **pup**. Pups are born without fur so the roost must be dry and warm. The mother bat hangs upside down, while the pup clings to her 'right side up', to drink her milk. If the colony is in danger, the mother may carry her pup to a new roost. By the end of July, the pup starts to fly and catch insects for itself.

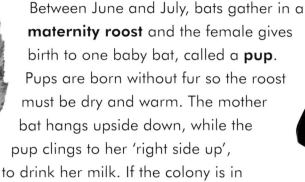

Lesser horseshoe bat

Left: Leisler's bat. During the day, bats sleep, hanging upside down. Just before sunset, they leave their roost to hunt for insects in woodland, over farmland, rivers and lakes.

ECHOLOCATION

Bats use their special hearing to find their dinner in the dark. They emit high-pitched calls that humans can't hear. These calls bounce off objects and echo back to their sensitive ears, allowing them to build a picture of their surroundings. This is called **echolocation.**

DID YOU KNOW?

11 species of bat **have been recorded in Ireland.**

One pipistrelle bat can catch over **3,000 midges** in one night!

Bats may travel 3km from their roost in a single night, looking for food.

ABOUT ME - BAT

My Irish name: Ialtóg/sciathán leathair, which means 'leather wing'.

Size: I am very small, 4–20g. Some Irish bats are so small they could fit in a matchbox!

Life span: 40 years or more.

Speed: 15kmph in complete darkness!

I like to eat: Insects and spiders.

BUTTERFLIES AND MOTHS

Summary is butterfly and moth season.

Common blue

BUTTERFLIES

Summer is when most butterfly caterpillars transform into flying adults. The main focus for the adults is to mate and lay their eggs. You can see butterflies visiting flowers to drink nectar from inside the flower.

Red admiral

THE 4 STAGES OF A BUTTERFLY LIFE CYCLE

A butterfly lays tiny eggs on a foodplant. Each egg hatchtes into a caterpillar. The caterpillar is a mini-eating machine and grows bigger and fatter. What happens next is one of the true wonders of the natural world. The caterpillar weaves a **chrysalis** and turns into a pupa. Inside, it transforms into a butterfly. After about 4 weeks, the adult butterfly emerges with crumpled wings that it spreads out to dry. It can now make its first flight and sets out to find a mate. And the whole cycle begins again.

DID YOU KNOW?

Ireland has 33 species of butterfly. Butterflies usually lay their eggs on the foodplant their caterpillars will feed on when they hatch out. They leave their babies right at the dinner table where they can feed and grow!

A peacock butterfly emerging from its chrysalis after metamorphosis.

NETTLES ARE NICER THAN YOU THINK!

Many butterflies and moths lay their eggs on nettles so their caterpillars can eat their leaves. The beautiful small tortoiseshell, peacock and red admiral butterflies all lay their eggs on nettles, so it is a good idea to leave a patch of nettles in our gardens, local parks and school grounds.

Garden tiger moth

White plume moth

MOTHS - DID YOU KNOW?

Did you know there are over 1,200 different moth species in Ireland and many are very beautiful?

Many moths visit gardens after dark and are attracted to pale, night-scented flowers, to drink nectar.

Some moths, such as the six-spot burnet moth (below right), fly during the day.

The hummingbird hawk moth (below left) is an amazing-looking insect and gets its name because it hovers like a humming bird.

Hummingbird hawk moth

Six-spot burnet moth

SUMMER ON OUR WETLANDS
Wetlands are very special places for wildlife in Ireland.

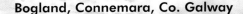

Bogland, Connemara, Co. Galway

BOGLAND

A bog is a lovely place to visit in summer. Bogs are home to insects, amphibians, birds, mammals, and a host of plants found nowhere else, such as the insect-eating **sundew**.

Bogs take many thousands of years to form and once they are gone, they are gone forever. A lot of the bogland in the world has disappeared, so this makes Irish bogs even more precious.

Bogs are home to the Irish hare, smooth newt, and common frog (See page 14), and insects such as dragonflies and damselflies.

Bogs also provide habitat for beautiful birds, including curlew, snipe, hen harrier, meadow pipit and skylark. In the summer months you may not see the skylark, but you will hear it! As it sings non-stop from the skies above an Irish bog.

A killer plant! The sundew gets nourishment from insec that become trapped on its sticky leaves!

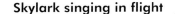

Skylark singing in flight

Hen harrier

Snipe

POND LIFE

Early summer is the best time to go pond-dipping.

Dragonfly

Pondskater

Tadpoles

Water boatmen

Water scorpion

Diving beetle

Newt

Dragonfly nymph

DID YOU KNOW?

There are 11 types of **damselfly and** 13 types of **dragonfly in Ireland.**

FLYING DRAGONS

Dragonflies and **damselflies** are beautiful wetland insects. Damselflies are small and delicate, about 3cm long, while dragonflies are larger, up to 7cm long. Damselflies hold their wings together when resting on a plant, while dragonflies spread them out.

Dragonflies and damselflies can be seen between May and September. The adults mate in the summer, and the female lays her eggs on the water or on water plants. The eggs hatch into **nymphs** that live underwater in wetlands, rivers and lakes, feeding on small animals, over the next few years. Then they crawl out of the water and onto a plant stem where they **moult** into an adult dragonfly.

Four-spotted chaser dragonfly

Damselfly

35

AMPHIBIANS AND REPTILES

In Ireland we have one type of native toad, one lizard and one newt.

NEWT

The smooth newt, like the frog and the natterjack toad, hibernates through winter. In April, it makes its way to ponds to breed.

The male newt develops a bright orange belly with spots on the underside and performs an underwater dance to attract females.

The female lays her eggs on underwater plants, wrapping each egg inside a living leaf.

The eggs will develop into larvae, called **efts**, and at the end of the summer, they will leave the pond as miniature newts.

ABOUT ME - SMOOTH NEWT

My Irish name: Earc sléibhe.
I look a little like a lizard but I am an amphibian, like a frog – which means that I am cold-blooded and I begin my life in water but spend most of it on land. I am nocturnal.
I like to eat: Meat! As an eft, I ate tiny water animals and insect larvae. As an adult I eat insects, small snails, slugs, worms and spiders.
Size: 10cm from head to tail tip.
Home: Dark, damp places in wetlands, fields and ditches.

TOAD

Our only Irish toad, the **natterjack toad** breeds in May. The female lays eggs in long strings. The tadpoles develop into young toads before leaving the breeding pond and moving onto land, where they spend most of their lives.

ABOUT ME - TOAD

My Irish name: Cnádán.
My body: I have warty-looking skin and I usually walk or crawl, rather than hop.
Size: I am about 7cm long.
I like to eat: I start life as a vegetarian, eating algae and plants. Later, I eat beetles, slugs, snails and worms.
Home: Sand dunes and ponds.
Sounds: I croak very loudly. You can hear me and my friends from miles away during the breeding season in May.

Natterjack toads are rare in Ireland. They are only found at about 12 coastal sites in Co. Kerry and one site in Co. Wexford.

LIZARD

The common or viviparous lizard is our only native reptile. The best time to see lizards is early in the morning when they are basking in the sun. Because lizards are cold-blooded, they need to heat up to become active.

DID YOU KNOW?

The common lizard can shed the end of its tail if caught by a predator, so the confused predator is left with just a tail as the lizard runs off!

The viviparous lizard gets its name because unlike most reptiles, it gives birth to live young instead of eggs.

ABOUT ME - LIZARD

My Irish name: Earc luachra.

My body: I am 10–16cm long and covered in scales that are grey, brown, copper or green.

I like to eat: Insects, spiders, snails, slugs, and worms. I pounce on my prey and shake it to stun it before eating it whole!

Home: Grasslands, bogs, sand dunes, cliffs, and rocky places such as the Burren.

Do we have a snake in Ireland after all? No, it's not a snake. It's actually a legless lizard called a slow worm that was brought to the Burren region by people in the 1970s and still lives there.

NEW LIFE ON OUR COASTS

Ireland has over 3,000km of coastline and hundreds of offshore islands for nesting seabirds.

During the summer months, seabirds, such as puffin, gannet, cormorant, shag, razorbill, fulmar, and guillemot rear their young around the Irish coast and on our offshore islands.

Razorbill

Fulmar

Rathlin Island, Co. Antrim

GRAND DESIGN

Guillemots don't build a nest. They rest their egg on their large feet, like penguins do. The male and female take turns at egg-minding, passing the egg from one to the other. The shape of a guillemot's egg is more pointed than other birds' eggs. This means that if it rolls, it rolls in a tight circle and is less likely to fall off the cliff edge. Before guillemot chicks can fly, they must jump off the cliff to reach the water far below!

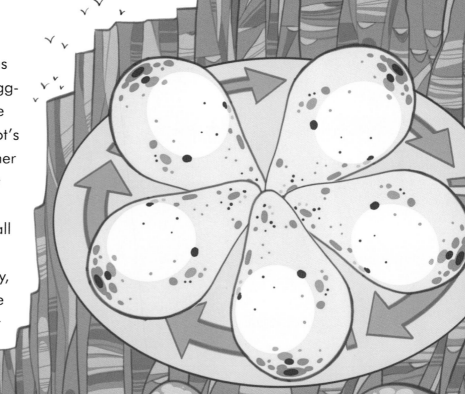

Black-backed gull

Kittiwakes

Guillemots

Cormorants

Puffins

PUFFIN

As this lovely little seabird waddles around on land, it might remind you of a penguin.
Underwater it looks like it is flying as it chases fish.

Puffins spend most of the year far out to sea, and only come to land each summer to mate and rear their chicks in a **burrow**.

DID YOU KNOW?

Puffins pair for life, and return to the same burrow each year.

Baby puffins are called pufflings.

ABOUT ME - PUFFIN

My Irish name: Puifín.
My body: I have a brightly coloured bill and large orange webbed feet that help me to swim.
I like to eat: crustaceans and fish, especially sandeels.

THE FORCE AWAKENS!

Each summer, gannets gather in large, noisy colonies on rocky islands to breed and lay their eggs. Skellig Beag (Little Skellig) in Co. Kerry, one of the locations for *Star Wars*, is home to over 30,000 gannet nests each year. With so many birds, the whole island looks snow-capped in summer.

A gannet chick

DID YOU KNOW?

Gannets usually return to the same nest site each year.

To catch fish, the gannet plunges headfirst, like a dagger, into the water. Flying up to 40m above the waves, it folds back its wings, stretches out its neck, and dives, reaching speeds of up to 120kmph, and diving up to 10m below the surface.

ABOUT ME - GANNET

Irish name: *Gainéad.*

My body: I am Ireland's largest seabird – I have a wingspan of over 2m. My extra thick skull acts like a crash helmet to protect my brain from the violent impact as it hits the water. I also have special throat pouches that inflate like airbags to protect my body when I dive.

Home: I spend most of the year at sea but return to the same nest site each summer to raise my chicks.

ARCTIC TERN - GLOBAL TRAVELLER

Roseate, Sandwich, Common, and Little terns spend the summer in Ireland, but the Arctic tern has made the longest trip to get here.

A LONG, LONG WAY

Arctic terns travel from as far south as the Antarctic to as far north as the Arctic and back again in winter – so they lap the globe each year, travelling about 32,000km!

It's summer all year round for the Arctic tern. First they spend summer in the southern hemisphere, then they come north to enjoy our summer, and raise their chicks before heading south again in September. What an amazing journey these young chicks face! The Arctic tern has the longest migration of any creature on the planet!

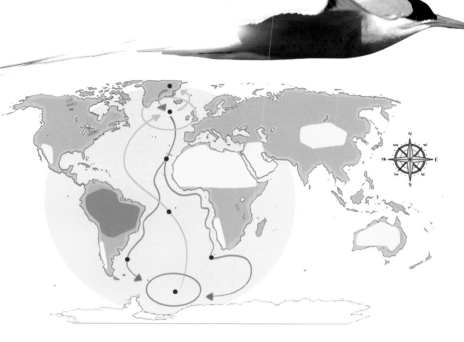

DID YOU KNOW?

Migrating birds change altitude **(or height) to find the best wind conditions.**

To fight a headwind, birds fly low, close to hills, buildings and trees.

To ride a tailwind, they fly high with the wind.

Counties Wexford, Kerry, Mayo and Donegal have the largest number of Arctic terns.

You can see them at Lady's Island Lake, near Rosslare, in Co. Wexford.

UP, UP IN THE AIR

Another amazing long-distance traveller, the **swift** comes to Ireland to breed in summer. After the chick leaves the nest, it flies without landing for up to 3 years; it drinks, eats and sleeps on the wing, only returning to land to raise its chicks!

OUR GIANTS OF THE DEEP

Whales, dolphins and basking sharks can be seen off the Irish coast.

WHALES, DOLPHINS AND PORPOISES

Summer is a good time to try to spot whales, dolphins and porpoises from a clifftop or to take a whalewatching boat trip. These are marine mammals; they breathe air and the females produce milk to feed their babies.

DID YOU KNOW?

25 different types of whales and dolphins have been seen in Irish waters.

HUMPBACK WHALE

The humpback whale migrates from cold polar regions to warmer breeding areas closer to the equator to give birth. Many swim over 20,000km each year. They feed close to land and can be spotted feeding off the Irish south and west coast.

Humpback whales are known for **breaching** – jumping straight out of the water. Scientists are not sure why they do this – it may be to communicate with each other; it may be to knock little animals and parasites off their body, or it may be just for fun!

Humpback whale off the south-west coast

Breaching humpback whale

Common dolphin often follow boats, riding the waves created by the bow or front of the boat.

Bottlenose dolphins are very playful animals.

DID YOU KNOW?

When a baby dolphin or whale is born, its mother pushes it up to the surface so that it can take its first breath of air. It breathes through its blowhole – the special nostril on top of its head.

ABOUT ME – BASKING SHARK

Irish name: *Liamhán gréine or ainmhí sheoil* (which means the 'beast with the sail').
Size: 6–8 metres long.
Weight: 6 tonnes.
My body: I don't have proper teeth. Instead I have gill rakers to sieve plankton from water.

GIANT SHARKS

The 8m-long basking shark is the second largest fish in the world (second only to the whale shark) and is a gentle giant. Like the large baleen whales, it feeds on tiny animals and plants called **plankton**. It swims along with its huge mouth wide open, filtering seawater through its gill-rakers, which trap the plankton. Every summer, basking sharks feed off the coasts of counties Donegal, Mayo and Kerry, gathering at spots where currents concentrate plankton on the surface.

DID YOU KNOW?

In just one hour, more than 2,000 tonnes of seawater passes through the mouth of a basking shark. That's the same volume as a 50-metre swimming pool!

MUTE SWAN

During the summer families of swans can be seen on lakes, rivers, and canals.

The Claddagh, Galway City

The mute swan is one of our most beautiful birds. It is one of the heaviest flying birds in the world. When it takes off, it has to run along the surface of the water to get airborne – like a large plane travelling down the runway. Landing is even more challenging. It must stretch out its feet and skid along the water until it stops.

ABOUT ME - MUTE SWAN

My Irish name: *Eala bhalbh.*

Weight: About 11kg.

I like to eat: Grasses and underwater plants.

Home: We build our large nest near water, using reeds, rushes and other plants. We often use the same nest year after year.

DID YOU KNOW?

Despite its name, the mute swan does make sounds. It snorts loudly and hisses if disturbed, especially if it has eggs or chicks to protect.

The male swan is called a **cob** and the female a **pen**. They stay together for life.

Swan chicks are called **cygnets**. They enter the water one or two days after hatching and are able to swim and feed on plants straight away. The mother often helps them by pulling up deeper plants and placing them on the surface. The fluffy, grey cygnets sometimes hitch a ride on the male's back.

LITTLE AND LARGE

The egg of the mute swan is the largest of any Irish bird, measuring over 110mm long and 70mm wide!

The tiny goldcrest lays eggs that are only 13mm long, by 9.5mm wide. How can a baby bird hatch from something this small!

The goldcrest is Ireland's smallest bird, weighing just 5g (less than a 20c coin!), and measuring 9cm from its beak to the tip of its tail.

WILDLIFE FUN IN SUMMER
Summer is a good time to get out and about.

HOLLY JO

OUT ON THE WATER

Take a **whale-watching** boat trip around the coast, especially along the south and west. The Irish Whale and Dolphin Group organise Whale Watch Day each August, and experts can help you observe these marine mammals from clifftop locations all around Ireland. (See www.iwdg.ie)

Visit a **seabird colony**. You could see puffins, gannets, guillemots, kittiwakes, razorbills or fulmars.

ROCK-POOLING

If you visit a beach this summer, check out the life in the rock pools. (See page 58.)

POND-DIPPING

Visit a local pond and see what insects and small fish you can find. (See page 35.)

Centipede

Spider

Beetle

WHAT TO SPOT?

Go on a mini-beast safari. Look under pots, stones, wood, and in leaf litter to see decomposers, such as centipedes, woodlice and beetles, at work.

Woodlouse: The woodlouse is not an insect but a crustacean. He is more closely related to lobsters and crabs than insects! Woodlice eat rotting plants and wood.

Earwigs: Male earwigs use their pincers to fight each other, but they have no interest in your ears! They come out at night and rest during the day under rocks and logs. Earwigs eat dead plants and small insects. The earwig is a very good mother. She is one of only a few insects who protects her eggs until they hatch.

Woodlouse

Earwig

Earthworm: Earthworms are very important to us all. They eat dead plants and help to mix the soils. Without worms, we wouldn't be able to grow crops!

Ants: Ants make their nests under soil or stones. You usually see ants crawling about on the ground, but in summer you may see a swarm of flying ants! This is when ants are born with wings and fly off to mate and set up new homes. When they have found a good patch, they shed their wings as they won't need them anymore.

Earthworm

Ants

MIDNIGHT SAFARI

Explore your garden after dark with a torch. Rainy nights will bring worms to the surface, and you will find snails and slugs feeding on the plants. Their slime trails help them to move. In the morning, you can follow the trail and see where your slugs and snails have been.

DID YOU KNOW?

A snail is both male and female at the same time. After two snails mate, both lay eggs. A snail's eyes are on the end of its long feelers on its head.

WILDLIFE WALKS AND TALKS

Heritage Week takes place at the end of August with wildlife talks and walks. (See www.heritageweek.ie)

Try an organised bat walk with **Bat Conservation Ireland**. Bat experts will show you how to use a bat detector. You can eavesdrop on the ultrasonic calls of bats that humans can't hear and identify different bats.

AUTUMN

Autumn is a time of plenty, allowing birds and mammals to stock up for winter.

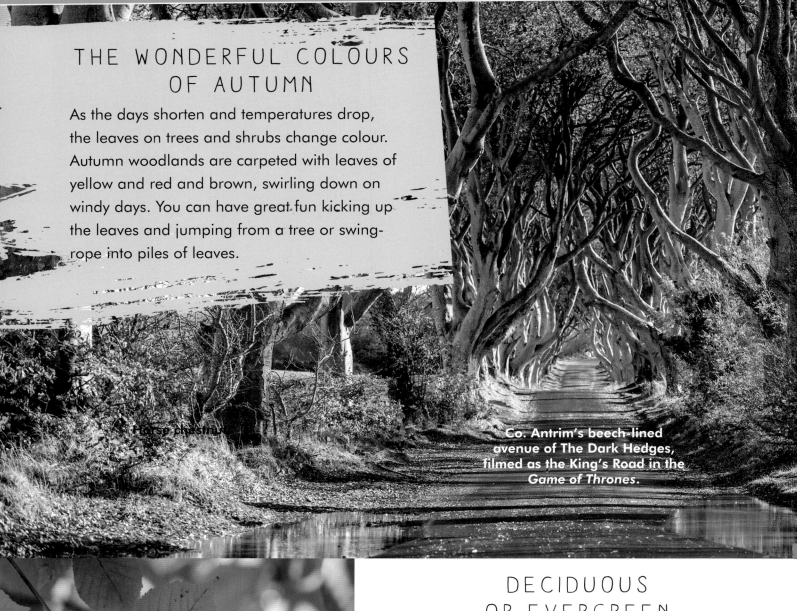

THE WONDERFUL COLOURS OF AUTUMN

As the days shorten and temperatures drop, the leaves on trees and shrubs change colour. Autumn woodlands are carpeted with leaves of yellow and red and brown, swirling down on windy days. You can have great fun kicking up the leaves and jumping from a tree or swing-rope into piles of leaves.

Horse chestnut

Co. Antrim's beech-lined avenue of The Dark Hedges, filmed as the King's Road in the *Game of Thrones*.

DECIDUOUS OR EVERGREEN

Deciduous trees are trees that lose their leaves every autumn. Evergreen trees stay green all year round. They usually have smaller leaves – like tough green 'needles'.

Evergreen
holly

Deciduous
hazel

ARRIVALS AND DEPARTURES

Our summer visitors leave for warmer destinations. Swallows and house martins can be seen gathering in large numbers, lined up on telephone wires before they leave.

Other birds arrive on our shores in autumn. Barnacle geese fly all the way from Greenland, a distance of over 2,000km, while many small birds, such as starlings, and waders, such as curlews, come here from mainland Europe because of our mild winters.

Why is a tree like a big dog? They both have a lot of bark!

Curlew

Brent geese also migrate to Ireland from the High Arctic in Canada.

49

AUTUMN IN THE GARDEN

Our gardens, hedgerows and woodlands offer a bounty of food.

FEAST TIME

In autumn many birds switch their diet from insects to seeds, nuts and berries, such as blackberries, rosehips, elderberries, rowan berries, hazelnuts, chestnuts and acorns.

Hazelnuts

Horse chestnuts (conkers)

DID YOU KNOW?

The wood mouse can climb branches to reach the tastiest berries. Like squirrels, wood mice store nuts in the ground for winter and some grow into new trees!

WHY DO LEAVES CHANGE COLOUR?

Inside a leaf there are millions of little packages of colour in green (**chlorophyll**), yellow (**xanthophyll**) and orange (**carotene**, the same colour as in carrots).

In summer, the green chlorophyll packages get energy from the sun, carbon dioxide gas from the air, and water from the plant roots and through a process called **photosynthesis** they make **glucose** (a type of sugar) which is food for the tree. When autumn comes we have shorter days and less sunlight so the green packages in the leaves shut down and then we see the yellow and the orange and sometimes red and purple if sugar gets trapped inside the leaf. Then the tree closes off each leaf and the leaves die and fall off. It's almost like the tree shuts down or goes to sleep for winter!

Rowan berries: Thrushes love the red berries of the rowan tree.

Blackberries: Even foxes and badgers enjoy blackberry picking in autumn!

Haws: (Below right) The hawthorn/whitethorn is a common sight in our hedgerows with its masses of red haws.

Sloes: The blackthorn's dark fruits are called **sloes**.

Berries: A favourite of small mammals, tits and finches.

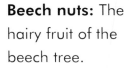

Beech nuts: The hairy fruit of the beech tree.

Acorns: Produced by our oak trees, acorns are a favourite food of squirrels, small mammals and many birds.

RED SQUIRREL

Squirrels live in woodlands, hedgerows, parks, and might visit your garden.

ABOUT ME - RED SQUIRREL

My Irish name: *Iora rua.*
I like to eat: Seeds from pine cones, nuts, buds and shoots; as well as berries, fruit and mushrooms.
Where do I live? I build a round nest called a drey, using twigs and bark, high in the branches or in holes in trees. I line the drey with moss, leaves and grass. I sleep here and it is home for my babies, called kits.

AUTUMN

Autumn is the **busiest time** for squirrels. They collect as much food as they can and bury it or hide it in trees for the winter.

WINTER

When the weather is cold and there is less food around, the squirrels can just dash to their hiding places and pick up their 'fast food' and then run back to their cosy nest. In winter, the red squirrel's fur coat gets thicker and redder in colour, and its tail gets more bushy to help protect it from the cold. On top of its ears, the red squirrel grows long **ear tufts** in winter.

SPRING

In spring, **courtship** includes high-speed chases as males try to get the attention of females. They can be spotted chasing each other up and down the trunks of trees.

SUMMER

The female squirrel usually gives birth in the drey to a litter of 3–6 **babies** between May and August. They are born blind and have no fur so they stay inside for about 9 weeks. The mother comes and goes, feeding her babies. When they are 9 weeks old, they start to explore their treetop home. With their long claws and good sense of balance they are good climbers from this young age. They have to be!

DID YOU KNOW?

We have two types of squirrel in Ireland: the native red squirrel and the grey squirrel.

Squirrels are diurnal; they are usually active during the day and they sleep at night.

A squirrel can leap from branch to branch, like an acrobat. It holds out its long bushy tail for balance.

A red squirrel might bury thousands of nuts each autumn. Some of these hidden seeds are never used and they grow into new trees the following spring.

Another animal that stores food is the **jay**, a beautifully coloured type of **crow.** The jay hides thousands of acorns for winter. Like all crows, it is very clever so it can remember where it hides food.

53

FUNGI AND LICHENS

Lots of mushrooms and toadstools appear in autumn.

FUNGI

Fungi live all year round as a mass of fine threads under the soil and put up their fruiting bodies (mushrooms) in autumn as a way of reproducing. Instead of using seeds, fungi release **spores** into the air. Fungi do not photosynthesise like plants to make their energy. They feed on organic matter in the soil or they live on dead or living plants or animals.

This bracket fungus lives on an old tree stump.

Fly agaric is a beautiful, but poisonous, red toadstool – the one in fairytales.

Lichen on a branch.

LICHENS – TWO ORGANISMS IN ONE!

A lichen is a fungus and an **alga** that are in a **symbiotic relationship**, helping each other to survive. The fungus provides structure and protection for the alga, and the alga makes the nutrients and carbohydrates that feed the lichen. There are 1,200 types of lichen in Ireland. They are sensitive to pollution so the cleaner the air the more you see.

Lichen

DID YOU KNOW?

Most fungi live underground as long thin strands spreading through the soil. We only notice mushrooms and toadstools when they send up their fruiting bodies above ground.

If you were able to weigh all the underground fungi in a woodland, it would probably weigh the same as all the trees of the woodland!

SPOT ME, IF YOU CAN!

Some of Ireland's mammals are *very* difficult to spot.

PINE MARTEN

The pine marten is a beautiful agile animal that spends much of its life in **trees**. It has a chocolate-brown fur coat. Its long claws help it to climb, and it moves easily up and down trees and jumps from branch to branch.

DID YOU KNOW?

The pine marten often has a number of dens in its territory and may travel 20km in one night as it searches for food.

IRISH STOAT

The stoat is a curious animal and a **master hunter**. It has a long slim body and is very fast. It is able to squeeze through small gaps. It can chase small mammals into their burrows and will follow over long distances until it catches its prey. The Irish stoat is a unique type to Ireland and does not turn white in winter.

ABOUT ME – PINE MARTEN

Irish name: Cat crainn, means 'tree cat'.

I like to eat: Small mammals, birds, berries, mushrooms, worms, insects, and frogs.

Home: I make my den in hollow trees or behind rocks, in large birds' nests or squirrel dreys. I line it with dried grass.

GREY SEAL COLONY

From autumn to early winter, grey seals come ashore to breed.

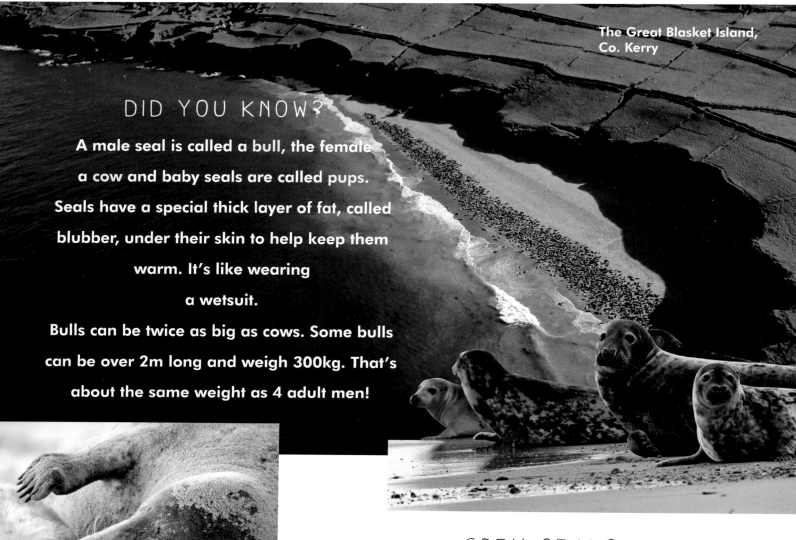

The Great Blasket Island,
Co. Kerry

DID YOU KNOW?

A male seal is called a bull, the female
a cow and baby seals are called pups.
Seals have a special thick layer of fat, called
blubber, under their skin to help keep them
warm. It's like wearing
a wetsuit.
Bulls can be twice as big as cows. Some bulls
can be over 2m long and weigh 300kg. That's
about the same weight as 4 adult men!

**A grey seal pup has creamy white
fur when it is born.**

GREY SEALS

In autumn, hundreds of grey seal cows gather on our offshore
islands, in **seal colonies**, to have their pups. The cows return to
the same beach every year. Grey seals communicate using lots of
noises – growls, grunts, hisses, barks and roars. So a seal colony is
a noisy place!

The mother stays close to her pup for the first few weeks of its life.
The pup grows very quickly. Its mother's milk is very rich in fat. By
about 3 weeks it is 3 times the size it was when it was born. Now,
with a good fat store, it moults and gets a new **waterproof** fur
coat, and goes to sea to learn to catch fish for itself.

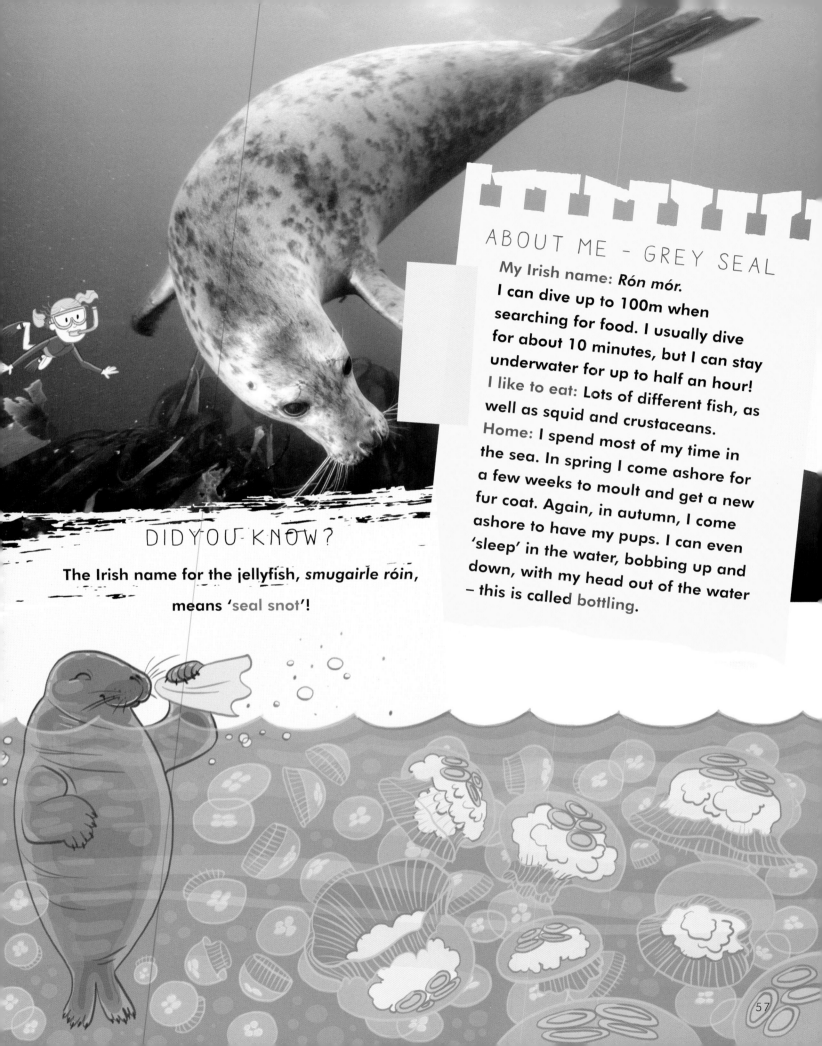

ABOUT ME – GREY SEAL

My Irish name: *Rón mór.*

I can dive up to 100m when searching for food. I usually dive for about 10 minutes, but I can stay underwater for up to half an hour!

I like to eat: Lots of different fish, as well as squid and crustaceans.

Home: I spend most of my time in the sea. In spring I come ashore for a few weeks to moult and get a new fur coat. Again, in autumn, I come ashore to have my pups. I can even 'sleep' in the water, bobbing up and down, with my head out of the water – this is called bottling.

DID YOU KNOW?

The Irish name for the jellyfish, *smugairle róin*, means 'seal snot'!

LIFE IN A ROCK POOL

Explore the underwater world of rock pools.

WHAT TO SPOT ON THE ROCKY SHORELINE

When the tide goes out, some amazing creatures stay trapped in rock pools.

The **hermit crab** moves into the empty shell made by another animal and carries it around to protect its soft lower body. (Spot him in the pool on page 59.)

If you have ever tried to pull a **limpet** from its rock, you know how difficult it is. But did you know this strong little creature moves around, eating algae, when the tide comes in and after dark? It always returns to the same spot before the tide goes out or before daylight.

Limpets

DID YOU KNOW?

A starfish sticks out its stomach to digest its food. When it catches a mussel, it prizes it open with its strong sucker feet and sticks out its stomach through its mouth and pushes it inside the mussel shell to digest the animal inside. Luckily humans don't have to eat like this or restaurants would be very different places!

Barnacles

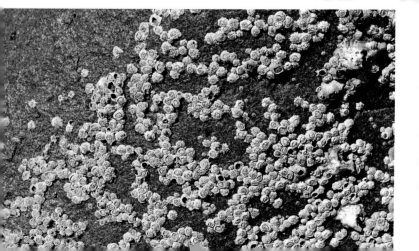

Barnacles are those little grey lumps you see on rocks at the beach. They are actually crustaceans, like crabs and lobsters, that look a little like tiny volcanoes. Once they attach to the rock as tiny baby barnacles, they never move for the rest of their lives! When the tide comes in, feathery legs come out of the tip of the barnacle to catch tiny animals in the water.

An **anemone** has tentacles it sticks out into the water when the tide comes in. If a small fish swims closeby, these tentacles can grab and sting it.

SEAWEED

There are lots of different types of algae or seaweed. They come in all different shapes and sizes, and can be green, red or brown.

Bladderwrack (See right) is one type of seaweed you might see on the shore. The bladders are filled with gas to help the seaweed float so that it can catch sunlight, which it uses to make energy.

The leaf-like part is called a **frond**.

Mussels

Dog whelk

Shrimp

Starfish

Anemone

Hermit crab

59

RED DEER

The red deer is our largest land animal.

DID YOU KNOW?

The male red deer is called a stag. The female is called a hind and the young are called calves. The hind does not grow antlers and is smaller than the stag.

A stag's antlers are shed each spring and a new set starts to grow. They are fully grown by September!

Each year the antlers grow larger, with more points or tines.

Deer antlers are the fastest growing tissue of any mammal, and can grow two and a half centimetres in one day!

DEER RUT

Red deer are shy creatures that will hide if disturbed. Stags and hinds live in separate groups except at rutting time. The **deer rut**, when the stags compete to become boss, is one of the most dramatic spectacles of autumn.

SHOWING OFF

The stags wallow in the mud, making large puddles, called **wallow holes**, so they smell strongly. They also thrash their antlers against plants and wear the vegetation that hangs from their antlers like a crown. They roar deeply in a vocal contest with other stags.

THE FIGHT

If none of this showing-off works, they must **fight**. The stags clash their antlers together and push each other in a test of strength. The strongest stag becomes the boss of the herd and the father to the calves born the following summer.

ABOUT ME – RED DEER

My Irish name: *Fia rua.*

I like to eat: I love grass, but I also eat herbs, acorns, woody shoots and fruits.

Home: I live in lots of places around Ireland, but you might see me if you visit Glenveagh National Park in Co. Donegal or Killarney National Park in Co. Kerry.

A deer rut – fighting stags

Sika deer

Fallow deer

SMALL BUT DEADLY

While the red deer is our largest land mammal, Stags weighing 200kg (200,000 grammes, about the weight of three adult men!), the **pygmy shrew** is the smallest, weighing only 4 grammes.

ABOUT ME – PYGMY SHREW

My Irish name: *Dallóg fhraoigh.*

I like to eat: Bugs, beetles, spiders and woodlice. Because I am so small I lose my body heat quickly and I have to eat all the time to keep warm and stay alive. I hunt day and night and eat my own body weight in food every day; that's about 200 bugs!

Home: Anywhere I can hide in ground cover and find food to eat – grasslands, hedgerows, woodlands and your garden.

WILDLIFE FUN IN AUTUMN

Have wildlife fun in school and after school or at weekends.

WHAT TO DO

Nuts, berries and autumn leaves: Crunch through the fallen leaves and collect some treasure for your classroom Nature Table. Make a scrap book or picture with leaves, adding the name of the tree and where and when you collected it.

Deer: Join a guided walk in the Phoenix Park in Dublin to see fallow deer, or visit places like Killarney National Park in Co. Kerry to see red deer. Don't get too close to male deer as they are very big animals with large pointy antlers!

Get your school buzzing. Ask your teacher to sign up to the All-Ireland Pollinator Plan to help our bees by growing wildflowers. (See www.pollinators.ie)

BAT BOXES

Putting up a bat box on walls, posts or tree trunks offers a safe place for bats to roost.

DID YOU KNOW?

A strand of spider's silk is stronger and tougher than a strand of steel.

Spiders' webs: Autumn is the best time to spot spiders' webs. When grass and hedgerows are wet with dew in the early morning, you can see lots of webs.

All spiders use **spider silk** to create webs. A single spider can produce up to 7 different types of silk which it can use in different ways. It may use one type of silk to create a web and another to wrap its eggs into a cocoon.

A spider makes a new web every day! Sometimes you see single strands of web on long grass or hanging from your ceiling – these are **guide lines** used by spiders to make a fast exit or to find their way home!

Acorn

DID YOU KNOW?

If every school planted an Irish tree, that would mean 3,305 new trees!

If every primary school teacher planted a tree that would mean 32,000 trees.

If every primary school child planted a tree that would be half a million new trees for Ireland's wildlife!

You can collect tree seeds such as acorns and conkers to grow your own trees.

A bug hotel

PLANT A TREE

Planting a native tree (such as an oak tree) is a great way to help Irish wildlife.

A BIODIVERSITY FLAG FOR YOUR SCHOOL

Make your schoolyard a safe **haven** for wildlife in your area. (Visit www.greenschoolsireland.org)

ROCKPOOLING

Take a trip to the beach and see what wildlife you can find or make a school trip with a wildlife guide. (For rockpooling tips see pages 58-9.) The Heritage in Schools Scheme has a list of wildlife experts. (See www.heritageinschools.ie)

BUG HOTEL

Make or buy a **bug hotel** to offer homes to hibernating insects.

WINTER

Days are short and nights are long and cold.
Animals have different ways of coping with the cold.

Winter ice at the lough in Cork city.

Some animals store food in autumn that will see them through the coldest months; many grow thick winter coats of fur; while some sleep right through winter. Some leave the country, flying to warmer lands. Others must stay at home in Ireland, working hard to find enough food each day through winter.

OUR SMALL BIRDS

Robin

Winter can be a tough time of year for small birds, as food is scarce and they must use a lot of energy just to stay warm. You often hear people talk about the 'fat robin', but in winter robins are far from fat. They are actually puffing out their feathers to try to stay warm!

WINTER VISITORS

Winter is a great time to visit bird reserves and mudflats at the coast. (See map for some of the many place to visit.) Here you will see huge flocks of waders carefully probing for worms and shellfish in the mud at low tide. Some of these birds have come to Ireland to spend the winter, from continental Europe and as far away as Greenland and the High Arctic.

SNOWDROP

The **snowdrop** is one of the first flowers to appear – as early as January or February. Snowdrops grow from bulbs underground, sending up hard-tipped shoots that can break through even frozen soil and snow!

WINTER FOOD

Ivy is a very important plant for birds, as it is one of very few plants to produce berries during winter.

INSECTS

Many insects die off before winter comes, leaving their offspring to spend winter as eggs or larvae until the spring comes. The queen bees and queen wasps survive by **hibernating** through winter.

Some butterflies migrate to warmer lands. The painted lady flies all the way to Morocco in North Africa.

DID YOU KNOW?

Did you know common wasps make their nest out of paper? Over winter you may discover the remains of an old, empty wasp nest in a shed or garage. If you take a closer look, you will see how the wasps made the nest walls using paper, which they make using chewed wood.

WINTER IN THE GARDEN

**During our coldest season, why not make your garden or schoolyard
a restaurant for wild birds?**

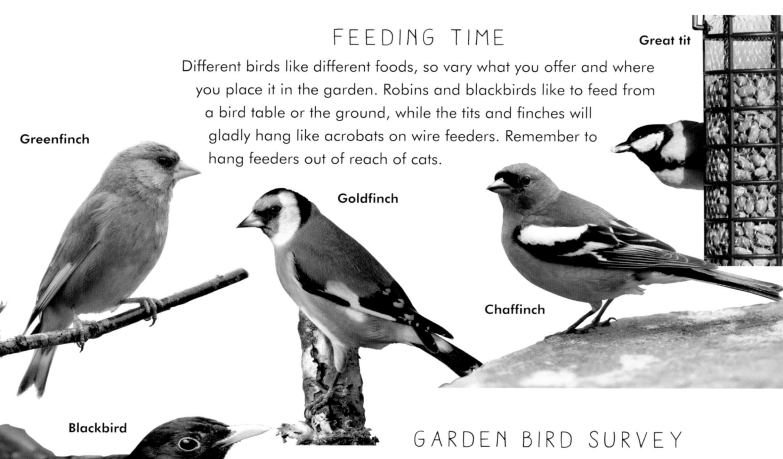

FEEDING TIME

Different birds like different foods, so vary what you offer and where
you place it in the garden. Robins and blackbirds like to feed from
a bird table or the ground, while the tits and finches will
gladly hang like acrobats on wire feeders. Remember to
hang feeders out of reach of cats.

Great tit

Greenfinch

Goldfinch

Chaffinch

Blackbird

GARDEN BIRD SURVEY

BirdWatch Ireland runs a Garden Bird Survey and if you take part,
you will learn to identify most common garden birds and some
more unusual visitors. (See www.birdwatchireland.ie)

**Grey squirrels like to visit
bird feeders too.**

CLEVER CROWS

Crows are one of our earliest nesters. As early as February, you will see rooks and magpies carrying twigs in their beaks, as they start to gather nesting material. It is easy to see the large nests of crows high in the trees at this time of year when there are no leaves.

Rook

Magpie

DID YOU KNOW?

The 'crow' family includes rook, raven, jackdaw, carrion crow, hooded crow, chough, magpie and the colourful jay.

Crows are known for their intelligence, problem-solving and communication skills. Crows have the largest brain to body ratio of all birds!

GREY HERON

The grey heron is another early nester. In January or February, it builds its nest high in the treetops. Before they build their nest, the male and female herons clap their bills together. Then the male heron presents a branch to the female to start building their nest.

ABOUT ME - GREY HERON

My Irish name: *Corr réisc.*
I'm also called 'Long Tall Sally' or 'Molly the Bog' in Ireland.
Size: At almost 1m tall, I am Ireland's tallest bird.
I like to eat: Fish, frogs, and anything I can catch!

DID YOU KNOW?

The grey heron usually nests alongside other herons. We call this a heronry. A heronry might be home to 50 heron nests, and have been in use for over 100 years.

HIBERNATION

Some animals have a clever way to survive winter – they go to sleep.

Hibernation is a special type of sleep – when an animal's body temperature drops **very** low and their heart rate slows down – so they can use very little energy.

HEDGEHOG

In October or November, the hedgehog looks for a good hibernation nest site, under a pile of leaves or at the base of a hedge.

During hibernation, its body temperature drops to about 4°C and its heartbeat slows from over 200 beats per minute to just 5 beats per minute. This means it won't need to eat, and can live off its stored body fat until warmer spring weather arrives. It usually doesn't wake up until March or April!

DID YOU KNOW?

Baby hedgehogs are called hoglets!

Your body temperature is around 37°C.

Imagine it dropping to 4°C, like the hibernating hedgehog. That's the temperature when water starts to freeze! Brrrr!

ABOUT ME - HEDGEHOG

My Irish name: *Gráinneog* means 'horrible one' or 'ugly one'!

I like to eat: Insects, worms, caterpillars and fruit. I'm known as the gardener's friend as I love to eat slugs and snails, which eat garden plants.

Each night I walk up to 3km while I search for food.

My body: My face and belly are soft, so if I get scared I roll into a ball so my 5,000 spines protect me!

BATS

Bats hibernate from November to late-March. Hibernating allows them to survive when there are few flying insects for them to eat. They hibernate in cool, humid hiding places – such as caves, mines, walls, roofs or hollow trees – where they let their body temperature drop to that of their surroundings.

Hibernating animals need to build up enough fat stores in late summer and autumn to see them through winter. A bat stores fat between its shoulder blades.

FROGS

Frogs seek out frost-free spots, in rock piles, under wood or tree stumps, where they sleep from October to January. Our other amphibians, the smooth newt and natterjack toad also hibernate.

INSECTS

Lots of insects become dormant or hibernate through winter. You may find a butterfly inside your home in winter, which looks dead but they might just be in a deep sleep. The small tortoiseshell, peacock, comma, and brimstone butterflies all overwinter as dormant adults. Other butterflies overwinter as eggs or pupae.

Migrant swans, geese, waders and other birds arrive in Ireland from colder lands.

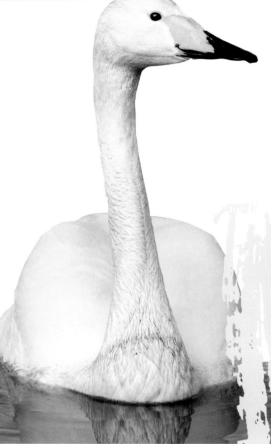

WHOOPER SWANS

Each October **whooper swans** fly all the way from Iceland to Ireland to spend the winter in our milder weather. The swans breed in Iceland and raise their chicks before migrating. For this year's cygnets the long journey must be quite a shock! The family group stay together for the migration and most swans choose the same spot on an Irish lake or river each year to spend the winter months.

DID YOU KNOW?

This is a long-distance migration, a return trip of over 2,600km, and is probably the longest flight undertaken by any swan. Whooper swans can live to 25 years of age, which could mean 25 return trips between Iceland and Ireland, or flying over 60,000km in a lifetime!

You can tell the difference between a mute swan and a whooper swan by their bills. The whooper swan has a yellow and black bill, and the mute swan has an orange bill.

A whooper swan was recorded flying at 8,230m, making it Ireland's highest flyer!

ABOUT ME - WHOOPER SWAN

Irish name: *Eala ghlórach* means 'noisy swan'!

I am much noisier than the mute swan, which lives in Ireland all year round. I make a honking trumpeting call.

I like to eat: Grasses and water plants.

WHOOPER SWANS, BRENT AND BARNACLE GEESE MIGRATION

Greenland

Iceland

BRENT GOOSE

BARNACLE GOOSE

BARNACLE GOOSE

BRENT GOOSE

WHOOPER SWAN

Ireland

Brent geese fly to Ireland from the High Arctic in Canda through Greenland to enjoy our milder winters. You can see them grazing on football pitches and park lawns.

Barnacle geese also come to Ireland to spend the winter, staying here from October to March. They fly all the way from Greenland. A large population overwinters on the Inishkea islands, Co. Mayo.

DID YOU KNOW?

Long ago, people believed that barnacle geese disappeared into the ocean each summer, because they looked like they were flying to nowhere. Then they would fly back from the sea the following autumn. Some people even thought these geese hatched from the barnacles on the seashore! This is how they got their name.

WINTER WADERS

MUDFLATS

In winter, you will find waders on the mudflats, at our coasts and estuaries, searching for food. While the tide is out, they dig up worms and shellfish with their special bills.

The **oystercatcher** has a bright orange bill and red eyes.

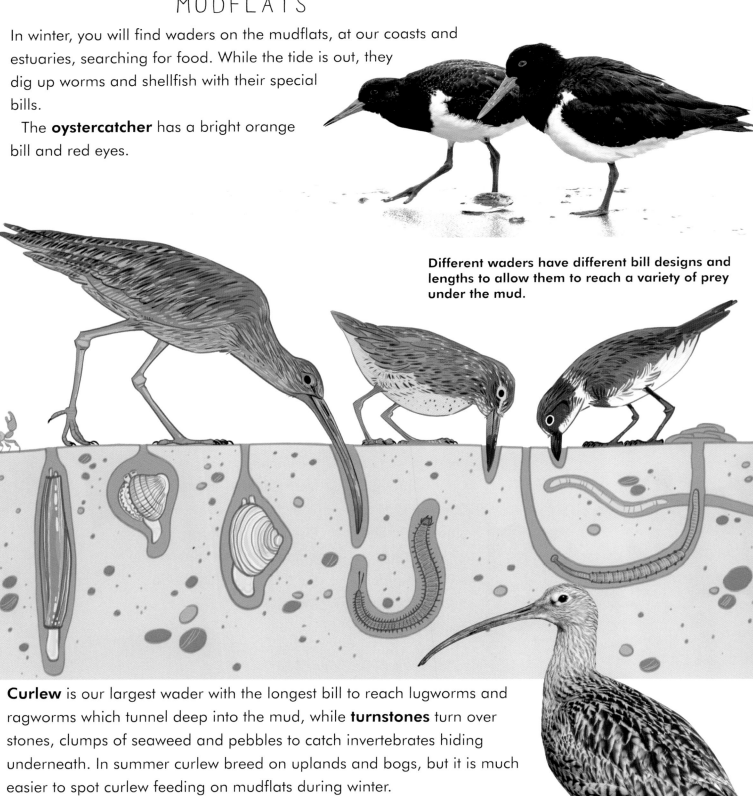

Different waders have different bill designs and lengths to allow them to reach a variety of prey under the mud.

Curlew is our largest wader with the longest bill to reach lugworms and ragworms which tunnel deep into the mud, while **turnstones** turn over stones, clumps of seaweed and pebbles to catch invertebrates hiding underneath. In summer curlew breed on uplands and bogs, but it is much easier to spot curlew feeding on mudflats during winter.

The **lapwing** is a beautiful bird with a long curved crest of feathers on its head, and green feathers on its back.

Dunlin are the most common wader in Ireland, forming flocks of thousands of birds.

Knot can also form huge flocks.

NATURE'S MISSILE

In winter, the fastest animal on the planet is often seen around our coast hunting wader flocks. The **peregrine falcon** can reach 300km per hour in its hunting stoop. It flies over its prey, then it dives like a missile from the sky.

GULLS
DID YOU KNOW?

There is no such thing as a 'seagull'. There are lots of different types of gull, and many live and feed inland. Black-headed gulls are often seen with jackdaws and rooks following a tractor as a field is ploughed, looking for worms. The herring gull is our most common gull. It breeds at the coast but will also nest on rooftops in towns near the coast. Common gulls breed on islands in lakes and head to coasts in winter. Lesser black-backed gull and great black-backed gull breed on coastal islands and rocky cliffs. Kittiwakes also nest on coastal cliffs and islands and spend the winter months far out at sea.

ATLANTIC SALMON

**There are many legends about the salmon, including the
story of the 'Salmon of Knowledge'.**

Salmon river on the Dingle Peninsula, Co. Kerry

THE CYCLE OF LIFE

The salmon spends the first two years of its life in Irish rivers. Then, it swims down
the river towards the coast to begin an amazing journey out into the Atlantic
Ocean. Its body must change from living in freshwater to living in salt water.
It turns north and swims towards the very cold waters of the **Arctic
Circle**, where it will find the best food that will help it
grow into an adult.

When it has grown, it will begin
its journey back to Ireland
to breed. Each
salmon will go back
to the same river
where it hatched
years before.

SPAWNING

In late December, the migrating salmon arrives at its destination – the stream of its youth. Tired and battered from leaping obstacles and swimming against strong currents, it still has an important job to do.

It must produce the next generation of young salmon. This is called **spawning**.

The female digs a bed (called a **redd**) with her tail in the gravel at the bottom of the stream. She lays her eggs and they are fertilised by the male. The female covers the eggs with gravel and leaves them to hatch.

In a few years they will follow their ancestors' out to sea and return to spawn in this same stream of their birth.

Salmon must leap over many obstacles, such as weirs and waterfalls on their journey upstream.

ABOUT ME - SALMON

Irish name: *Bradán.*

I like to eat: Young salmon eat insects, invertebrates and plankton. Adults at sea eat other fish, squid, eels, shrimp and krill. But once I return to freshwater from the sea, I don't feed again. I swim hundreds of kilometres, leaping weirs and waterfalls, and spawn – all on an empty stomach!

DID YOU KNOW?

Scientists have found that some Irish salmon travel over 3,000km. No one knows how the salmon find their way back to Ireland from the Arctic. Some scientists think salmon might be able to smell the stream where they hatched from vast distances.

One salmon can lay over 10,000 eggs.

A MURMURATION OF STARLINGS

One of winter's most wonderful wildlife spectacles.

AERIAL DISPLAY

Starlings are common birds. You see them in gardens and parks, chattering away together, all year round. But in winter, starlings put on an amazing display called a **murmuration**.

At this time of the year starlings form huge flocks and they sleep or **roost** together in a reedbed or patch of woodland. Fifty thousand starlings roost together each year under a bridge in the centre of Belfast!

As the starlings come in to roost for the night, they don't go straight to bed. Instead, they fly in close formation, making a dark moving, swirling cloud of flapping wings in the sky – like a super-organism.

Starling

STARLINGS ARE GO!

DID YOU KNOW?

Nobody knows how starlings manage to fly like this, but perhaps that makes it even more exciting to watch!

A flock of 50,000 starlings have 100,000 eyes watching for danger. So if a sparrowhawk or another bird of prey fancies starling for dinner, he will be spotted the minute he appears. Flying in these tight groups also confuses birds of prey.

Another good reason to join a flock in winter is for warmth. Small birds lose heat very quickly. It is important not to waste energy in simply keeping warm. So starlings and many other birds roost together at night.

Pied wagtails also roost together in large numbers in winter – often on trees in cities – to share their body heat and the heat given off by traffic, streets and our concrete buildings at night.

Rooks and jackdaws roost together in trees in large groups over winter. We call this large roost of crows a rookery.

WILDLIFE FUN IN WINTER

It might be cold out there but there's still plenty to see and do in winter.

Winter in the Wicklow Mountains

WHAT TO SPOT

Tracks and signs: If we do get a snowfall, look for animal tracks left overnight by nocturnal animals. Other signs include nibbled nuts or pine cones or pellets of unwanted food coughed up by owls.

Squirrels: January is a great time to see squirrels. There are no leaves hiding your view and they are particularly frisky this month. You might even see a couple of squirrels playing kiss-chase at high speed as they race around the trunk of a tree.

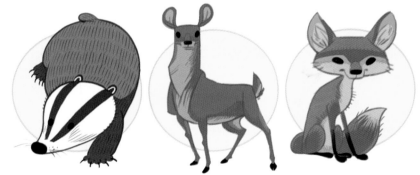

Early nesters: From the start of February, keep an eye out for rooks, magpies and grey herons carrying sticks and nesting material. Blackbirds also start to build their nests in February.

Rookery: Visit a rookery in the evening to experience the noisy rooks and jackdaws as they bed down for the night.

Waders: Head to your nearest estuary to check out the wintering wading birds and wildfowl feeding at low tide. (See page 72.)

Little egret

SOME TIPS FOR WATCHING WADERS

➤ Wear waterproof, warm clothes.
➤ Bring binoculars if you can and a good bird book.
➤ Check the tide times online. Find a good spot an hour before high tide and you'll see the birds as they come closer with the tide, and then spread out over the mudflats as the tide goes out.

THINGS TO DO

Join Birdwatch Ireland. A birding trip with an expert is a great way to learn to identify birds and birdsong. (See www.birdwatchireland.ie for trips.)

Feed the birds: For tips, have a look at page 66.

Put up a nestbox: Nestboxes in your school or garden are a great way to offer new nest sites. Do so before the middle of February, as this is when birds will be scouting for homes.

Listen to the birds: Winter is a good time to identify bird songs as there are fewer birds singing. Those that sing all year round include the robin, great tit, wren and song thrush.

Dedication
For Joe x

Acknowledgements
Thanks to: Zoe Devlin, Cepa Giblin, Conor Kelleher, John Lusby, Dr Una FitzPatrick and Steve Newton
for support, encouragment and help with fact checking.

First published 2018 by
The O'Brien Press Ltd,
12 Terenure Road East, Rathgar,
Dublin 6, D06 HD27, Ireland.
Tel: +353 1 4923333; Fax: +353 1 4922777
E-mail: books@obrien.ie.
Website: www.obrien.ie
The O'Brien Press is a member of Publishing Ireland.

ISBN: 978-1-84717-915-9

10 9 8 7 6 5 4 3 2 1
22 21 20 19 18

Printed and bound in Poland by Białostockie Zakłady Graficzne S.A.
The paper in this book is produced using pulp from managed forests.

Published in
DUBLIN
UNESCO
City of Literature

Image copyright details:
All illustrations © Barry Reynolds. Photographs: pp8-9 (bluebell flower and background), 10 (fox cub), 12-3 (primroses, dandelions, cow parsley, lesser celandine, speedwell, buttercup), 33 (nettles), 48 (pine cone), 51 (haws, sloes), 54 (bracket fungus), 58 (starfish, rockpool), 65 (ivy, wasp nest), 67 (crow nests), 69 (frog), 79 (nest box) © Juanita Browne; p45 (swan, top) Elaine Browne; pp9 (mayfly), 16 (hare, bottom), 31 (lesser horseshoe bat), 42 (humpback whales, bottom, both), 55 (stoa), 56 (grey seals on Blaskets), 70 (whooper swan in flight & grazing), 73 (herring gull), 75 (salmon eggs) © Crossing the Line Films; p62 (bat boxes) © Conor Kelleher; p16 (hare, top) © Andrew Kelly; cover (red admiral), pp32 (red admiral & common blue), p33 (garden tiger moth, 6-spot burnet moth, hummingbird hawk-moth, white plume moth) © Liam Lysaght; pp7 (Glenveagh National Park), 20-1 (Shannon) © Carsten Krieger; p46 (whale-watching) © Daniel Lettice; p31 (Leisler's bat) © Martin McKenna; p9 (Maybug), 35 (damselfly and dragonfly) © Brian Nelson. All other photographs are courtesy of Shutterstock.
If any involuntary infringement of copyright has occurred, sincere apologies are offered, and the owners of such copyright are requested to contact the publisher.

WILDLIFE GROUPS AND USEFUL WEBSITES

All-Ireland Pollinator Plan, www.pollinators.ie
An Taisce - the National Trust for Ireland, www.antaisce.org
Bat Conservation Ireland, www.batconservationireland.org
Biodiversity Week, www.biodiversityweek.ie
BirdWatch Ireland, www.birdwatchireland.ie
ECO-UNESCO Conserving the environment, empowering young people, www.ecounesco.ie
Heritage Council, www.heritagecouncil.ie
Heritage Week, www.heritageweek.ie
Irish Garden Birds, www.irishgardenbirds.ie

Irish Peatland Conservation Council, www.ipcc.ie
Irish Whale and Dolphin Group, www.iwdg.ie
Irish Wildlife Trust, www.iwt.ie
National Biodiversity Data Centre, www.biodiversityireland.ie
National Parks and Wildlife Service, www.npws.ie
Royal Society for the Protection of Birds, www.rspb.co.uk
Ulster Wildlife Trust, www.ulsterwildlife.org
Wildfowl and Wetlands Trust, www.wwt.org.uk
Wildlife Rehabilitation Ireland, www.wri.ie
Wildflowers, www.wildflowersofireland.net

WILDLIFE HOTSPOTS
Islands, Wetlands and Where to See Giants of the Deep

Rathlin Island

Belfast Lough RSPB Reserve

Lough Barra Nature Reserve

Castle Espie Wetlands Centre

Lough Neagh

Ballybay Wetlands Reserve

Inishkea Islands

Girley Bog

Clare Island

Ireland's Eye

Clara Bog

Bog of Allen

Lough Borra Parklands

Pollardstown Fen

Abbeyleix Bog

Shannon Estuary

Wexford Wildfowl Reserve

Tralee Bay Wetlands Centre

Saltee Islands

Blasket Islands

Skellig Islands